Between Heartbeats

Between Every Moment, a Story

Myra Rao

BookLeaf Publishing

India | USA | UK

For my mom and sister,
whose love has been the heartbeat of my life,
and for all who continue to persevere,
finding strength in the face of life's challenges.

Preface

Between Heartbeats is a journey through the tangled landscapes of life. It is a collection born from the spaces where we all dwell: the moments in between the dramatic peaks and valleys, the quiet pauses when we feel most human. It is in these gaps that we experience the full spectrum of what it means to be alive—the joy that lifts us, the sorrow that pulls us low, and the quiet, everyday moments where everything else fades away.

The Gift of Rain

I asked the Universe for magic,
And the next morning,
I woke up to a gentle rain.

The soothing pitter-patters,
Raindrops trailing each other
On the glass windowpanes,
I felt love.

All the greens swaying
In the smooth breeze,
The monsoon gray
Spreading across everything you see,
I saw life.

The quaint scent of soil
as it breathes its fresh dew,
I smelled hope.

And then, suddenly,
I was healed.

I asked the Universe for magic,
And it answered with rain.

Simple Pleasures

Isn't life simple?
All we want is
a quiet space—
a pretty room of our own,
with a balcony that opens to trees,
if not a forest, then at least a glimpse
of something green, something alive.

We dream of moments with our people,
of laughter echoing in mountain air,
toes in sand, hearts full,
cuddled close under a moonlit sky,
where the world falls away,
and only joy remains,
dancing in the stillness of the night.

We want music that stirs us,
that makes us feel free,
and people who understand
that our freedom is ours to keep,
without apology, without fight.

We want love that stays,
love that isn't afraid to shout
its truth from the rooftops,
bold and unashamed—
because we would never be.

Spinning Rock

On the Days You Feel Less Than
Remember: we are all on a spinning rock,
shooting through darkness.
It's ridiculous—
and magical.
Your life is nothing short of a miracle,
your breath as radiant as the sun.

On the days you place your life in the "cons"
column,
remember:
you're measuring your worst
against everyone else's best.

When the world feels too heavy,
remember:
the air hums with miracles we often miss.
Bees waltz, sharing secrets of where flowers
lie,
butterflies taste with their feet,
and at dawn,
the birdsong stirs the trees from sleep.

The Warmth We Carry

I'm a little bit in love with all my friends—
the way we lean on each other,
no need for words,
just being together,
a silent comfort.
I'm in love with how we soak up each other's
presence,
like sunlight,
letting it fill us up
and hold us,
a warmth that stays long after we part.

I'm in love with the late-night phone calls,
when time slips away across the world,
and all that matters is the conversation,
the need to be heard.

I'm in love with the random meetups,
the long drives and trips,
just in time to escape the chaos
without even communicating the need.

I'm in love with the way they love—
with their kindness,
their laughter,
the way they leave pieces of themselves
woven into my heart,
a patchwork of moments.

A little bit in love with friendship,
with everything it gives—
the support, the joy,
the quiet understanding,
the way we make each other feel seen,
and never alone.

Home With a Story

You've crafted this space with care,
Each corner holding a quiet story.
Your favorite corner of the house, where
mornings unfold,
A cup of coffee, the world outside.

The things you've gathered—
An old vase, a book with worn pages—
They've found their place in the room,
Not just decor, but memories kept.

Nothing is rushed here,
You let the space breathe;
Each detail speaks softly,
Of who you are,
Of how you want to feel.

The sleekness soft, the edges bold,
A hint of luxe with threads of gold.
Not flashy, no—just full of flair,
A quiet elegance in the air.

You welcome guests with open door,
And they'll step in and feel the floor:
A dance of space, of light, of care,
A home that says, *I'm here, I dare.*

It's not about perfection,
But about comfort.
A home that welcomes,
Without needing to say a word.

At the Heart of the Table

Three women at the kitchen table,
laughter spilling like sunlight,
the kind of warmth that fills a room
and stays long after the words are gone.

Mom, still with the sparkle in her eye,
hands busy with something she's always
made—
a meal, a story, a little piece of home.
Her daughters, now grown,
but with the same grin,
the same tilt of the head,
the same comfort in her presence.

One with dreams that stretch like horizons,
always chasing new adventures,
while the other finds joy in the small things—
the quiet mornings, the steady rhythm of
routine.

But together, they are a perfect balance—
laughter, stories, love
swirling in the air like a song.
There's no need for words sometimes,
just glances,
just knowing.

The table feels full,
even when it's only the three of them,
because family is the place
where hearts are never too far
from home.

Woven From Many

Have we ever paused to notice that,
We are not just ourselves—
we are the echoes of everyone we've met,
a mosaic of voices, faces, and moments
woven together without us even noticing.

That song we love?
It's not just ours.
It's the one someone introduced
on an evening drive,
and we never forgot the tune.
That recipe we follow?
A roommate once shared it,
passing down a flavor
that's now ours too.

We have a corner in the city
that feels like home,
but it wasn't just luck—
it's the place where laughter once lived,
where a friend's smile shaped the space.

Our thoughts, too,
are made of borrowed wisdom—
a motto from a coworker,
a line that stuck
because it made sense,
so we kept it close,
like a small, secret compass.

We still tell that one joke,
the one we picked up from a classmate
on a Tuesday afternoon,
the punchline that never fails to land.

Our evening routine?
That's our father's rhythm,
the little rituals that made us feel safe,
and our mornings?
They're shaped by the calm of our mother's

voice,
setting the tone for the day.

What a wonder it is to know that
We are not singular.
We are the sum of every encounter,
each person who crossed our path,
leaving something behind—
a song, a habit, a smile,
a piece of who we are,
forever intertwined with theirs.

Someone

Someone I can groove to the tunes with,
Someone who can show me the meaning,
Someone who can hold my hand,
Someone who looks into my eyes, showing
love without words,
Someone who whispers sweet nothings,
Someone who blends with my soul,
Someone who gently tugs me to sleep.

Someone who means what they say,
Someone who listens without needing to
explain,

Someone with whom I can watch the stars,
Someone who I can dance the night away
with.

Someone to exchange music with,
Someone to laugh over memes with,
Someone to tease with gentle authority,
Someone who never lets go of my
authenticity.

Someone who can finish my sentences,
Someone who can fill my thoughts,
Someone who sweeps me off my feet,
Someone who lights up my dreams.

Before You Became Like Coffee

At first, you were just a smile,
familiar and fleeting,
a presence I didn't need
but found myself wanting.

Then, you became like coffee—
in the deliciousness,
and in the addiction.

I didn't know how much I craved
until I could no longer wake
without the taste of you.

Always, No Matter What

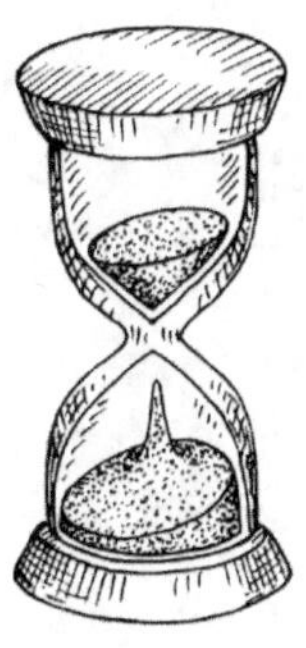

If everything I touch turns to gold,
can you be the ring on my left hand,
a token to mark the permanence,
the anchor in my ever-shifting world?
Or the locket around my neck,
staying close to my heart,
through every crest and trough,
so I can carry you with me, always?

If everything I touch turns into dust,
can you be the sand inside this hourglass,
sitting on my desk?
So I can admire you—

hour by hour,
grain by grain.

Without Question

If you are ever to be loved,
I hope it is painfully obvious,
Like the sun rising unashamed,
And the stars shining in the darkest nights,
A love that swells with certainty,
That doesn't whisper, but shouts your name.

A love that doesn't need to be measured,
No scale or standard to compare,
It is enough in its own weight,
And you know, without doubt, you belong there.
It doesn't linger in the shadows,
Hoping you'll find it,
It stands tall, arms wide,
Waiting for you to step inside.

A love that heals you to the core,
Not in a rush, but in soft waves,
It finds every scar and whispers,
"You are whole, you are enough."
It doesn't mend what's broken in haste,
But nurtures, until the cracks become
The places where light enters.

A love that blooms with no agenda,
It doesn't need to be "earned" or won,
It simply is, as natural as breath,
And as constant as the turning sky.
A love that grows in you,
Not in spite of who you are,
But because of all you've been,
And everything you still will become.

And when the world gets heavy,
When all else fades or falls apart,
This love will remain,
A thread, unbroken,
Binding you back to yourself,
A love that is clear—
And you never need to search for more.

A Little Longer

I sat on the endless shore,
listening to the sea's soft hum,
unable to ignore
how the waves, with quiet urgency,
keep running—
ebb and flow,
pulled and released
by the ocean's mighty reach.

But still, the shore remains,
patient, poised,
waiting,
with unspoken hope,
that for once,
the wave might linger—
soft and steady,
stay just a little longer,
or stay forever.

If patience is love,
nothing rivals the love of the shore.
If persistence is love,
nothing rivals the love of the waves.

When Leaves Fall

In English we say:
you were never mine....

In poetry, we say:
you were the high I chased
when I was at my lowest.
You were the leaves on my tree
when I needed roots.
You were my miseducation of love
and I...
your fool.

And so, I let you go,
like autumn lets go of its leaves.
With every falling,

I grow lighter.
No longer chasing the wind,
I am content to be the tree.

A Thousand GoodByes

Letting go isn't one clean break—
It's a thousand small goodbyes,
In the quiet moments between the noise.

You let go when their favorite dessert
Is on sale, but you don't buy it.
You let go when the scent of them fades
From the bottle you throw away.

You let go every year on the anniversary
of the day you lost them.
You let go when someone else holds you,
Or when the date slips by unnoticed.

You'll have to let go a thousand different times,
a thousand different ways,
Each time, again and again,
Not pathetic, not weak—

Just human, finding the pieces,
One goodbye at a time.

Exit Stage Left

Read me like a book,
Carry me like a song,
Remember me like a photograph,
Love me like a poet.

Let's dance one last night,
I'll exit the stage left, when
you are done.

Catching Myself

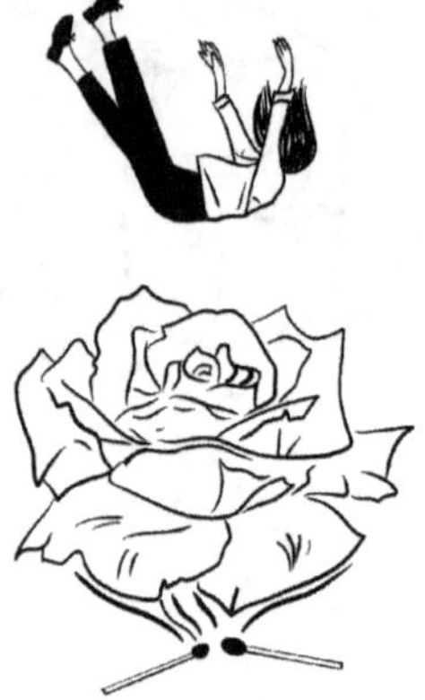

Let me fall, if I must fall,
Into the wild rush of wind,
The world spinning away like a dream
As I tumble through the air,
Unraveling, shedding layers
I never knew I wore.

The one I will become stands below,
With open arms, steady as the earth,
Not waiting to catch me,
But to meet me,
In the space between falling and rising,
Where everything shifts and nothing is lost.

So let me fall—
Let the ground rush up to greet me
With all its sharp edges and soft grasses,
For in this plunge, I will be reborn,
Not broken, but remade,
A wild thing learning to soar.

The Edge of Change

At the edge of comfort, where the world feels small,
There's a whisper of fear, a rise in the fall.
The unknown stretches, wide and bright,
A path untrodden, a blaze of light.

Excitement hums beneath my skin,
A tug to move, to shed what's been.
The old me lingers, soft and warm,
But something new is taking form.

I stand at the threshold, hesitant, unsure,
But something inside says, "You're meant for more."
The fear pulls back, the future calls,
A voice that shatters the familiar walls.

I take a step, then another, then run,
Reinventing myself, becoming someone.
Not who I was, but who I could be,
Unfolding the layers of possibility.

The fear is still there, like a shadow in light,
But with each step, it fades from sight.
Excitement wraps me in a warm embrace,
As I find my rhythm, my new place.

And in this journey, I start to see—
That stepping out is where I'm free.

Beneath The Surface

Before the storm, there's a quiet that we can't
ignore,
A weight in the air, but no one asks for more.
The world moves around, too busy to see,
The battles we fight, the things that defeat us.

When no one sees you fall apart,
Who's to say you touched the ground?
If a heart breaks in silence,
Does it even make a sound?

Every crack in the mirror, every tear in disguise,
A piece of us shatters, but no one realizes.
And though we're still standing, the cracks run so deep,
We carry the brokenness no one will ever see.

Almost Home

She waits beneath a tiny tree,
its shade a fragile shield from the sun,
waiting for the bus that takes her home—
mid-summer, in the scorching heat.

She was almost there—
or so she thought—
when suddenly,
she was dropped,
right in the middle of nowhere.
In that burning heat, just like that.

Perhaps in another time,
in another universe,
she lies beneath fields of flowers,

butterflies drifting over her cheeks,
the sun's heat nothing more than
a soft kiss on her skin.

There, she is loved just right,
by the ones who were meant to love her.
And here, in this moment,
she is enough.

As Much As We Breathe

"Hope!" she cried, almost laughing.
 "Of course we need it."

"But what if it always feels out of reach?" he
asked.

"Hope doesn't live out there. It never has.
We don't discover it in the sky, or even in
other people.
There, deep inside the oceans of your own
true self–
it lives.

She smiled as she continued,

"And, as much as we must breathe to go on,
we must hope."

Green Flags

People who speak tough truths gently.
The ones who notice the little things.
Big picture thinkers, dreamers,
And deep feelers, who don't hide their hearts.

Old souls with young spirits,
Goofballs who make you laugh without
trying.
Those who never make you choose between—
What's right for you, or what's easiest for
them.

The ones who listen to understand,
Not just to reply.
The friends who let you share your fears
And hold them with care.

Quiet good-doers,
Those who can admit when they're wrong,
Or when they simply don't know.
People who understand their privilege,
And people who aren't afraid to take the last
slice of pizza.

The ones who make you forget your phone,
And remind you that lovely things
Still exist, right in front of you.

My incomplete list of green flags,
what I call "Keepers."

The Wings Of Dreams

Hold fast to dreams,
For they are the winds beneath your wings,
The spark in your soul that keeps you
reaching,
When the world pulls you down.
They are the warmth in the coldest night,
A flame that never dies,
Even when the darkest shadows loom.

Hold fast to dreams,
For without them,
We are lost—
Wandering, waiting,
In a world stripped of color,

Where the heart forgets how to sing,
And the spirit, adrift,
Yearns for something to believe in.

So hold fast,
For dreams are the breath of life,
The pulse that makes us whole.
Without them, we are nothing but dust,
Scattered in a wind that never cares.
But with them,
We can rise. We can fly.

The Weight She Carries

It's her,
The one who learned early to hold the
world—
To balance expectations like plates,
To carry the quiet weight of responsibility.

The years pass, and with each one,
The weight shifts but never quite leaves.
She stands at the crossroads,
Alone, yet never less than whole,
Unraveling the idea that a title
Can define the woman she is.

Her life is not a race,
Not a measure of time or milestones,
But a journey lived in moments—
Each choice a step, each pause a breath.

She may carry burdens,
But she also knows how to lay them down,
To dance alone in the joy of her own rhythm,
To find freedom in being, just as she is.

She is not behind,
Not waiting for something to arrive,
For she is already living,
Already whole, already strong.

The world may ask why,
But she answers with a smile—
For it's not the weight she carries,
But the strength to keep walking,
That makes her who she is.

The Beauty Of Now

Joy isn't a distant dream,
It's the little sparks, the quiet gleam,
In the pause between a breath, a laugh,
In simple moments that make you feel alive.

It's in the things that light you up,
Even if no one else gets the spark,
Like dancing alone with coffee in hand,
Or laughing at a joke only you understand.

Life's a swirl, it's true, it's loud,
But happiness is found in the quiet crowd—
In moments small, in moments bright,
In letting go and feeling light.

So don't chase it like it's a race,
Just let it find you at its pace,
Happiness is never far away,
It's in the little things, day by day.

Quiet Years

A seasoned couple in the corner,
hands weathered, slow to move.
She stirs her coffee with careful grace,
he watches, content, from across the table.

Their words are few,
but there's a quiet in their gaze
that speaks of years
woven together like the threadbare fabric of
their coats.

The world rushes by outside,
but they are still,
sipping warmth,
sharing time.

In their silence,
there's a history only they know,
and a love that doesn't need to be spoken.

In the Grind

It began with quiet exchanges,
coffee stirred in half-lit rooms,
shared glances over the hum of emails—
strangers at first,
now threads woven deep
into the fabric of the day.

In the pulse of meetings and deadlines,
their presence became a soft constant,
a shared breath between the chaos,
a laugh at the end of a long afternoon,
a silence that spoke louder than words.

Unseen at first,
but now,
they are the ones who know the weight of
your hours,
who lighten the load
with the simple grace of knowing.

Not planned,
yet now,
they are your quiet family,
the ones who make the world feel less heavy.

Co-workers!

Where we belong

After years apart, the door swings open,
and there they are—
the aunt with her ringing laugh,
the uncle's quiet smile,
cousins now grown,
their voices a blend of strangers and family.

Grammy's chair sits empty,
but her presence hums softly in the room,
while parents, with graying hair,
still hold us close,
their hearts the anchor we always return to.

In their faces,
in the warmth of their touch,
home is not a place,
but a gathering of love,
unbroken, timeless.

She Was Always More

She was once a girl,
full of dreams that whispered
of endless possibilities—
a heart wide open,
eyes full of stars.

Then marriage came, soft and steady,
and she built a life around it,
around family,
tucking her own dreams away
into the quiet corners of her heart.

Years passed, the house grew still,
and with loss, the silence was loud.

But in that quiet,
something inside her stirred—
a spark of who she once was,
a woman rediscovered.

Slowly, softly,
she began to rise.
Not just as a mother, not just as a wife,
but as the woman I've always known was
there—
stronger now,
braver than she realized.

In the stillness,
she's finding herself again—
alive with possibility,
ready to dream once more.

To all the moms,
who carry this story in different shades:
thank you for being exactly who you are.

Let us remember that once, you too were a
girl—
wild, dreaming, full of light.

And we are so proud to see you grow
into the strong, beautiful woman you've
become.
Your journey is ours, too.

Her, My Mirror

You, with your wild eyes and untamed laugh,
always running just a step ahead,
while I linger in the quiet corners
of the world we built together.

I watched you grow—
like a flower in fast-forward,
your boldness blooming before I knew
how to catch up.

I've seen you fall and rise
with a grace I didn't know you had—

how, in your own way,
you've learned to stand tall
in a world that asks for everything.
And you give it anyway,
with your heart wide open.

You've always had the courage
to be exactly who you are,
to chase your dreams
with that fierce, unshakable heart
I sometimes envy.
But when the world feels heavy,
I know I'll find you there,
a little wild, a little wild-eyed,
but always, always with room for me
to sit beside you.

You're my reminder
that there's strength in softness,
courage in the quiet moments,
and no matter how far you go,
you'll always be my sister,
my little one.

Into the Dusk

The day slips away like soft evening light.
The air cools, carrying the scent of earth,
and I step outside,
feet meeting pavement,
ready to shake off the weight of hours.

The sky wears a quiet shade of blue,
a promise of peace in the fading sun,
and the world, slowed by dusk,
seems to exhale with me.

Each step is a small release,
like unbuttoning a tight collar,
the rhythm of my walk
matching the quiet pulse of the evening.

The trees stretch their shadows,
whispering secrets to the wind,

and I listen—
not for answers,
but for the simple grace of this moment.

I pass familiar sights:
a porch light flickering on,
a dog's distant bark,
the rustle of leaves,
the soft hum of the world unwinding.

In this moment,
there's only the path,
the fading sun,
and the peace of being here,
free for a while.

The "Not so Little" Things

A shower after the beach,
Coming home after being away for a while,
A good test score when you thought you
would fail,
A whole group laughing at your joke.

A smile in the middle of a kiss,
A compliment on the insecurities you hide,
Your comfort movie after a warm shower,
perfect bliss,
A win in finishing something just as the
microwave beeps wide.

Hearing someone laugh after they've cried,
Hearing that you were in someone's dream,
A kid drawing your picture,
Peeling an orange in one perfect piece.

Rapping the entire song just right,
Parking as the song fades out, just in time.
Being swept off your feet in a hug,

The way the room looks after cleaning, it
shines.

Falling asleep in a car,
waking up in the morning in bed, feeling
completely fresh.

All these moments, small and true,
Life feels good in the little things,
And it's enough to pull you through,
Enough to love this process of living.

Everything Is Okay, My Love

The most beautiful parts of your life, the real
happiness, the true essence,
will be found in many small, nameless
moments.
They are never explosive—
though the explosive moments do matter,
it will always be about the everyday, little
sparks.

The laugh of the love of your life,
the first time your child calls your name,
dancing the night away with your friends,
a sunset, mellow and beautiful,

a glass of wine while on vacation,
staring out at an ocean view.

But perhaps the fullest you will ever feel ,
is from that whisper through the dark, saying,
"Everything is okay, my love. I've got you."

Paper Boats

A quaint December morning, cool outside,
I curl up inside, wrapped in warmth,
Watching a squirrel nibble on something,
While the world outside is soaked in
monsoon clouds.

The weather feels so familiar—it takes me
back.
To the tropical rains of my childhood,
Where gray skies and green fields felt like
home.
The cool breeze, the way the trees swayed,
The sound of gusts that whispered calm into
my chaos.

Rain was always a friend then.
Holidays, school breaks, a quiet house,
Mom's hot fritters—crispy, warm,
Eating them with my sister, watching cable
TV,
As the rain tapped against the windows,
And thunder rumbled far away.

We made paper boats,
Racing them in puddles,
Competing, laughing, drenched in joy.
On the terrace, we danced in the drizzle,
Jumping in water that collected in forgotten
corners,
Fingers tracing the rain's thin lines,
Fascinated by how it fell, how it danced.

Now, the fritters are replaced by coffee,
Home is distant, tucked away in a faraway
country.
The sister, the family, replaced by new faces,
Roommates, friends, or sometimes, just me.

But the rain, it still calls me home.
Through the sliding glass door, I watch it fall,

And for a moment, I am a child again,
Back in the rain, back in the warmth of those
days.

Beyond the Horizon

Wanderlust,
escape,
a breath between worlds,
where roads stretch like rivers of light,
each turn a quiet promise.

Airports hum with possibility,
faces fleeting, destinations unknown,
as the world spins in a dance of arrivals and
goodbyes.
In every place, beauty unfolds—
mountains kissed by dawn,

oceans whispering secrets,
and cities alive with color and sound.

Lovely people weave through the journey,
smiles like sunrays in foreign lands,
their kindness a bridge across the distance,
connecting hearts in silent understanding.

It's not escape from something,
but a running toward
the soft thrill of the unfamiliar,
where every journey
unwraps a new kind of freedom.

What Cannot Be Written

I sat down to write a happy poem,
But then I remembered, everyone loves
The tortured soul, the poet's pain,
And some have said, "Happy poems suck."

Do poets dwell on sadness?
Not really. They find joy in every little thing,
For they are the ones who romanticize life—
Even in the simplest breath, they sing.

So why not write more poems of light?
I tried, but each verse became a love letter—
To you, to me, to the sky brushed with sunset
hues,
To the birds' soft song at the day's first light.

Each poem is a letter of grief,
To my father, to loved ones gone,
To the version of me that no longer fits,
To love, to loss, to all I've drawn.

Each poem is a letter of hope,
To the future me, the family I'll keep,
To friends who are family in all but name,
To a world where kindness still runs deep.

And then I realized—
There's nothing familiar in "I'm feeling good,"
No words left to say.
The sadness inside is a loud, echoing roar,

But happiness? It's silent, it stays.
Happiness doesn't need to be told,
It asks for no expression, no written line.
It doesn't clamor for attention—
It simply exists, still and fine.